WHILE
RUNNING WITH THE WOLVES

Rationalizations
FOR WOMEN WHO
DO TOO MUCH
WHILE
RUNNING WITH THE WOLVES

———— 🦢 ————

Allison McCune
AND
Tomye B. Spears

BOB ADAMS, INC.
Holbrook, Massachusetts

Published by Bob Adams, Inc.
260 Center Street, Holbrook, MA 02343

ISBN: 1-55850-380-3

Printed in the United States of America

J   I   H   G   F   E   D   C   B   A

This book is available at quantity discounts for bulk purchases
For more information, call 1-800-872-5627

Rationalization—(rash'en e liz A shen)—
the act of devising superficial rational, or plausi-
ble, explanations or excuses for one's acts,
beliefs, desires, etc., usually without being
aware that these are not the real motives.

Justification—(jus' te fi KA shen)—the act
of showing to be just, right, or in accord with
reason; vindicate; to free from blame; declare
guiltless; absolve.

Excuse—(ik SKYOOS)—to serve as an expla-
nation or justification for; a plea in defense of
some action or behavior.

Contents

3. HAVING IT ALL?

4. THE BEAUTY OF IT ALL

5. EXCESSES OR BUST

Birth of a Book

One day, Tomye called Allison to announce that she had just spent $400 on sheets for her new bed. Quite distressed, Tomye felt totally guilty about spending so much money on something so incidental, but she really loved the sheets. Anyway, considering their long history of expert rationalizing, Allison asked her whether she preferred to keep the sheets or return them. Regardless of Tomye's reply, Allison was prepared to deliver an ideal justification for this seemingly irrational "white sale" hysteria.

Well, Tomye kept the sheets, but more importantly, an idea was born. It occurred to these women that their effortless ability to persuade themselves to defy logic with their actions was an interesting phenomenon. Perhaps other Homo Sapiens would benefit from the insightful, zany and profound rationalizations, justifications and excuses that Tomye and Allison invent on a daily basis . . . and hence, this book . . . to help all you folks out there find just the right rationalization for each and every occasion.

Acknowledgments

Thank you to my parents, Al and Peggy McCune, my sisters Evelyn Hughes and Louisa McCune, and my brother Joe McCune for a lifetime of loving support. Thanks also to Don Craig and Jack Spiegel for not letting me rationalize giving up on the road to publication.

—A.M.

I'd like to acknowledge my parents, the late Lois Searcy and Tom Boykin—without them I wouldn't be here. Special thanks to my sister Scarlette for being so supportive and believing in this book from the beginning. Most of all, I would like to thank my husband, Jay, whose enthusiasm and encouragement helped me remain persistent and positive. You're the best and I love you very much. Lastly, to my daughter Sam, who will be born in May—I can't wait to hold you.

—T.B.S.

We would also like to give special thanks to Laura Morin, our editor, and Wayne Jackson, our sales manager, who have both put in many hours of hard work and have had unending enthusiasm for this little book.

—A.M. & T.B.S.

1

THE ROOT OF ALL EVIL

"I have been poor and I have been rich.
Rich is better."

— Sophie Tucker

RATIONALIZATIONS FOR
LIVING BELOW THE POVERTY LEVEL

🕊 No one can call me a yuppie.

🕊 I don't have to worry about my jewelry being stolen.

🕊 My in-laws don't stay with me when they come to visit.

🕊 It's a great weight-loss program.

🕊 I don't have to feel guilty about not saving.

🕊 No one asks to borrow money from me.

🕊 I like my mobile home—really!

🕊 Who needs money? I have my art.

🕊 I've acquired a taste for mustard and Wonderbread sandwiches.

🕊 I'm one with the land.

RATIONALIZATIONS FOR
CHARGING WHEN YOU KNOW YOU SHOULDN'T

🐛 I believe in instant gratification.

🐛 I "had" to have it.

🐛 It's the nineties, I can pay twenty percent more if I want to.

🐛 I'll pay it off next month.

🐛 I need to establish more credit.

🐛 My nails were wet and my credit card was handy.

🐛 Using my gold card makes me feel rich.

🐛 My other five credit cards were maxed out.

🐛 I wanted the 26¢ cash back bonus.

🐛 I was preapproved.

RATIONALIZATIONS FOR
ORDERING FROM CATALOGS

🐸 It's just like getting presents in the mail.

🐸 They have those one-of-a-kind items.

🐸 They accept all major credit cards.

🐸 I can order from the privacy of my very own couch.

🐸 I don't have to put on make-up.

🐸 It's low-effort gift shopping.

🐸 Those bathtub splash guards were an absolute necessity.

🐸 The operators have become my friends.

🐸 I automatically get put on every mailing list on this side of the equator.

🐸 It makes me feel like somebody out there likes me.

RATIONALIZATIONS FOR
BUYING A HOUSE

🐌 I can have "pride of ownership."

🐌 My friends will be green with envy.

🐌 I can have my own pool and Jacuzzi for my bon bon eating moments.

🐌 I'll get more preapproved credit cards.

🐌 I'll finally have a guest room so my friends won't have to sleep on the floor.

🐌 We'll have more assets in case we get a divorce. (Doesn't the wife always get to keep the house?)

🐌 I won't be making my landlord rich.

🐌 I won't have to listen to my next door neighbors banging their headboard against the wall.

🐌 I can finally have pets.

RATIONALIZATIONS FOR
RENTING AN APARTMENT

🐛 I have a problem with commitment.

🐛 I don't have to worry about what kind of grass I'm supposed to grow in my yard.

🐛 Having lots of neighbors makes me feel popular.

🐛 I like listening to the neighbors head-board banging against the wall.

🐛 There's no down payment. (I can deal with a security deposit.)

🐛 I'm not into "owning" anything.

🐛 When something breaks, I don't have to fix it.

🐛 The doorman looks like Mel Gibson.

RATIONALIZATIONS FOR
BUYING AN EXPENSIVE CAR

🐦 I needed a new image.

🐦 It was only 23% interest.

🐦 The payments were only slightly higher than my mortgage.

🐦 The color was to die for.

🐦 I won't have to make the first payment for six months. (By then I will have a great job and my life together.)

🐦 The two vanity mirrors had lights with a lifetime warranty.

🐦 I got two free tickets to Hawaii.

🐦 It will help me get more dates.

🐦 It's an investment.

🐦 The salesman looked like my doorman.

RATIONALIZATIONS FOR
GETTING TURNED DOWN
FOR A BANK LOAN

🐌 The loan officer was jealous of my expensive new car.

🐌 I didn't think my year-long soul searching trip to Peru would matter *that* much. (My boyfriend *promised* he'd pay my bills while I was gone.)

🐌 Unfortunately, they called the personnel manager to verify my employment. (Just because I wrecked her life by having an affair with her husband doesn't give her the right to wreck mine.)

🐌 They said my African juju beads were not sufficient collateral.

🐌 I thought that having fourteen credit cards maxed out showed consistency.

🐌 They said getting a loan for starting a nudist colony for the mentally ill was not a good enough reason.

RATIONALIZATIONS FOR
RUNNING UP A BIG PHONE BILL

🐌 I thought having the "friends and family" plan meant that my friends and family would pay the bill.

🐌 Well, I'm not going to be anal and keep a timer next to the phone.

🐌 Hey, it's cheaper than airfare.

🐌 The time just flies when you call those 900 numbers.

🐌 I just don't ever think about it while I'm talking.

🐌 I'm rich.

🐌 I'm poor (but I'm doing positive thinking about abundance).

🐌 This month's $400 phone bill is just a fluke, I'm sure.

🐌 I thought Candice Bergen was paying.

RATIONALIZATIONS FOR
BOUNCING CHECKS

🕊 I only bounce one or two a month.

🕊 Most people notice the expiration date (10/71) on my charge cards.

🕊 It's safer than shoplifting.

🕊 I'm helping to keep at least one bank employee securely employed.

🕊 It's an inherited trait.

🕊 I was broke and needed a heart transplant.

🕊 I still have checks in my checkbook, so I must have money in the bank.

RATIONALIZATIONS FOR
OPENING A SAVINGS ACCOUNT

- 🐦 My kids will be able to have an education. (I don't think the University of Swahili Hut Building will be so bad.)

- 🐦 I'll feel like I'm a responsible person.

- 🐦 I'll feel like I'm rich.

- 🐦 I'll feel independent (I don't think it really matters that I went from being supported by my parents to being supported by my husband).

- 🐦 I'll feel like an adult. (Finally!)

- 🐦 I'll get to buy what I want, when I want (and that is very important to me).

- 🐦 I can open more charge accounts and buy more "stuff."

- 🐦 I needed a new toaster.

- 🐦 I'm saving up for an expensive new condom—it comes with a penis attached.

RATIONALIZATIONS FOR
NOT HAVING A SAVINGS ACCOUNT

🐦 I could die tomorrow so I better spend the money now.

🐦 I'll get married in a few years and he'll pay all the bills (don't count on it).

🐦 I'd have to eat dinner at home more often and all I can cook is tomato soup.

🐦 I'm too young to be responsible.

🐦 Easy come, easy go.

🐦 The monthly fees are higher than my monthly check.

🐦 I'm a prostitute, and I don't want the tellers to know how little I earn.

🐦 My ex would demand joint custody.

🐦 I don't believe in sperm banks either.

RATIONALIZATIONS FOR
NOT PAYING TAXES

- It's too time consuming.

- I'll make it up next year.

- I'm a Republican.

- I'm a Democrat.

- I live in a trailer with a chain link fence—life's hard enough.

- I'd have to report my income.

- It's against my religion.

- With all these people, they'll never miss mine.

- I'm a minor goddess.

- I have a masters degree in logic, so I can't understand the forms.

- Why should I be the one honest person?

- I'll be dead before they catch me.

IT TAKES TWO

"I wonder what Adam and Eve think of it by this time."

— Marianne Moore [on marriage]

RATIONALIZATIONS FOR
BEING STOOD UP

🐦 He works so hard, I'm sure he's just tired (yeah, right).

🐦 He must be in a ditch on the side of the road somewhere. (He'd better be.)

🐦 Actually, I was just about to stand him up, so he saved me the trouble.

🐦 He was a jerk anyway.

🐦 I probably got the time wrong.

🐦 I probably got the date wrong.

🐦 Actually, I probably got the whole damn year wrong.

🐦 I really wanted to read my book, *Walden*, anyway.

🐦 Maybe I shouldn't have told him about that new study on aging ovaries. (Well, yes, it was only our second date.)

🐦 His parole board said no.

RATIONALIZATIONS FOR
STANDING SOMEBODY ELSE UP

🐸 I hate confrontation.

🐸 I was stuck in a terrible traffic jam, I got home and my goldfish was dead, and then I found the plumber in *my* bed with the maid.

🐸 I forgot. (Was that consciously or unconsciously?)

🐸 I didn't want to lead him on.

🐸 I think he needed some time alone, anyway.

🐸 I had to "find" myself.

🐸 My house burned down?

🐸 My dad always says men want the chase—so, hey, chase away.

🐸 I got married—to someone else.

RATIONALIZATIONS FOR
NOT GETTING INTO A RELATIONSHIP

🐌 He sells feminine hygiene products for a living (door to door)!

🐌 He lives with his mother. (He's 34 years old for pete's sake!)

🐌 His other wives walk four steps behind him.

🐌 His nickname is "master of the universe." (He nicknamed himself.)

🐌 He has a seven-foot boa constrictor and he lets it chase little bunny rabbits around his apartment.

🐌 He said, "I love you" on our second date (yeah, right).

🐌 Getting a job is against his religious beliefs.

🐌 His idol is Al Bundy.

RATIONALIZATIONS FOR
STAYING IN A DEAD-END RELATIONSHIP

- My dog loves him.

- I get lots of free meals.

- I'm really just waiting until I meet someone else.

- We have great sex.

- It's not his fault he was raised by a pack of wolves.

- Everything finally works in my apartment.

- He lives far away so we don't have to see each other *that* often.

- We have an "open" relationship—I'm open to other people.

- His best female friend is a lesbian.

- His cute younger brother is turning eighteen next year.

RATIONALIZATIONS FOR
GETTING MARRIED

🕊 I can be a bitch and he can't leave. (If he does, I get half of everything.)

🕊 There will always be someone there when I come home. (Don't count on it.)

🕊 I'll have sex on a regular basis. (Don't count on this, either.)

🕊 I won't have to look good every time he sees me.

🕊 He's rich. (So what if he has bad breath?)

🕊 His parents live in Nairobi.

🕊 I'll get a big diamond ring.

🕊 I'll have twice as many assets.

🕊 I'll have someone to go on trips with (and to pay for it).

🕊 I'll get to use his credit cards (mine are maxed out).

RATIONALIZATIONS FOR
NOT GETTING MARRIED

🕊 I don't live in a community property
   state.

🕊 He's had four previous wives.

🕊 His kids are older than me.

🕊 Forever is a *real, real* long time.

🕊 My mother is convinced he's the devil.

🕊 He likes bar soap and I want liquid and
   we just can't come to terms.

🕊 I'd have to pay half the bills—so much
   for the fairy tale.

🕊 He's a Virgo and I'm a Sagittarius—it
   would never work.

🕊 What if I meet someone better?

🕊 His dog and my cat don't get along.

🕊 It would be harder to kick him out of the
   house.

RATIONALIZATIONS FOR
MARRYING FOR MONEY

- The first time around I married for love and that was definitely the wrong reason.

- I'm sick of buying all my clothes from Laundromats.

- I know he's 5'2", weighs 320 pounds, and is bald, but my four figure weekly allowance makes him seem ten feet tall.

- He only wants sex once a month (so what if I have to dress up like Little Bo Peep)?

- "Work" is not in my vocabulary.

- I'm a product of the eighties.

- Love can't buy you a spree at Macy's.

- I can always divorce him and keep half.

- I'm worth it.

RATIONALIZATIONS FOR
HAVING A BIG WEDDING

- 🐦 My parents are paying for it.

- 🐦 I'll get tons of presents.

- 🐦 I'll be the center of attention for months.

- 🐦 I get to pick out everything I want and people will actually buy it.

- 🐦 I get to throw a huge party for all my friends.

- 🐦 I can have ten bridesmaids and look really popular.

- 🐦 I'll have lots of big, beautiful photos of myself.

- 🐦 I can be a bitch and everyone has to be nice to me.

- 🐦 Everyone will have to tell me how beautiful I am.

RATIONALIZATIONS FOR
HAVING A SMALL WEDDING

- I have to pay for it.

- I won't have to write as many thank-you notes.

- I won't have to invite people I don't like.

- Crowds make me crazy.

- I can't deal with a bunch of bitching bridesmaids.

- I'm three months pregnant and I don't have time to plan.

- My favorite church only seats 50.

- Everyone would know if I invited 500 people that I only wanted their presents

- There will be fewer witnesses if I throw up.

RATIONALIZATIONS FOR
ELOPING

🕊 I won't have to spend money on those stupid brides magazines.

🕊 It probably won't last long anyway

🕊 It's romantic.

🕊 It's a great opportunity to piss off his parents.

🕊 He has a bad case of acne and our photo album would be just terrible.

🕊 He needs his green card.

🕊 He's an ex-con.

🕊 I'm eight months pregnant and I ran out of time to plan.

🕊 I don't have any friends.

🕊 My parents think he's a Kennedy

RATIONALIZATIONS FOR
HAVING SEX

- I ate cheesecake for dessert and needed to work it off.

- For an instant, he reminded me of Kevin Costner and I wanted to go with the flow.

- I wanted to try out my new boob job.

- My name is Bambi. (What did my parents expect?)

- I wanted a promotion.

- I just stocked up on batteries.

- We heard the neighbor's headboard banging and it inspired us.

- He just bought me a diamond necklace and I owed him.

- I was bored.

- I ran out of excuses.

RATIONALIZATIONS FOR
NOT HAVING SEX

🐌 My rug burns haven't healed yet.

🐌 My moon is in the wrong house.

🐌 I just got off the phone with my mother.

🐌 The cats are watching.

🐌 I forgot to use my feminine deodorant spray.

🐌 My peek-a-boo maid's outfit is at the cleaners.

🐌 I ran out of rhinoceros horn powder.

🐌 His nose hairs were out of control.

🐌 I'm eight months pregnant and I really resent him.

🐌 I ran out of batteries.

RATIONALIZATIONS FOR
FORGETTING TO TAKE YOUR PILL

- ❧ I never got out of bed.

- ❧ I was mad at my husband.

- ❧ I wanted to lose weight.

- ❧ I was broke.

- ❧ I hate my job.

- ❧ I fell in love with a "Latin" who doesn't believe in birth control.

- ❧ Why take a pill every day if I only have sex once a month?

- ❧ I decided to become a nun.

- ❧ I decided to become a lesbian.

- ❧ My goldfish ate them.

RATIONALIZATIONS FOR
MISSING YOUR PERIOD

🐦 My periods are irregular anyway.

🐦 I was depressed this month.

🐦 My diet must have caused it.

🐦 My in-laws are staying with us.

🐦 I bounced a check (to the IRS).

🐦 I just found out my husband is having an affair (with my lover's daughter).

🐦 I've been suicidal a lot this month.

🐦 My hampster was recently diagnosed with a terminal disease.

🐦 I just had plastic surgery.

🐦 I'm probably sterile anyway.

🐦 I have a cold.

RATIONALIZATIONS FOR
TAKING A HOME PREGNANCY TEST

🐸 I got a coupon in the mail.

🐸 I'm going out tonight and I want to know if I can drink or not.

🐸 My husband's coming home tomorrow after being away for six months, and I need to know for sure.

🐸 I want to surprise my boyfriend at dinner tonight.

🐸 I need to know if I should start planning my wedding.

🐸 I like watching my boyfriend sweat.

RATIONALIZATIONS FOR
NOT TAKING A HOME PREGNANCY TEST

🐸 They can't be *that* accurate.

🐸 I don't want to know for sure.

🐸 I don't want to get married.

🐸 I don't want to think about it right now.

🐸 I only slept with him once.

🐸 His secretary told me he had a vasectomy.

🐸 I'm into denial.

RATIONALIZATIONS FOR
GETTING PREGNANT

🐸 I can eat anything I want and still have "the glow."

🐸 I look cute in maternity clothes.

🐸 I just turned 30.

🐸 My husband will do everything for me.

🐸 I can be a bitch and everyone has to be nice to me.

🐸 I can stay in bed and eat bon bons.

🐸 I'll have boobs for nine months.

🐸 I can eat pickled okra and sugar cookies at 2:00 A.M. and not feel one ounce of guilt.

🐸 It's a great rationalization for not exercising.

🐸 I won't have to worry about birth control.

🐸 I get to decide when and how much sex we have and he can't say no.

RATIONALIZATIONS FOR
NOT GETTING PREGNANT

🐸 I have a low threshold for pain.

🐸 I'm only 30.

🐸 My doctor says my sex drive will decrease. (If it decreases any more it will be gone.)

🐸 With my luck, I'll have a litter.

🐸 Children aren't in our five-year financial plan.

🐸 My thighs will never look the same.

🐸 My iguana fulfills my maternal instinct.

🐸 I have to have eight full hours of sleep.

🐸 The kid might look like my husband.

🐸 The kid might not look like my husband.

RATIONALIZATIONS FOR
HAVING CHILDREN

🐦 I'll have someone to talk to.

🐦 I'll have a miniature of me. (How perfect!)

🐦 I'll have a miniature of my husband. (How dreadful!)

🐦 They'll keep me young. (Maybe I won't have to have a facelift.)

🐦 Finally—someone to help with the chores!

🐦 I'll get to go shopping more often.

🐦 I'll get to bake tons of cookies (yummy).

🐦 I'll have someone to take care of me when I get wrinkled and senile.

🐦 It'll give me another reason to worry. (I live to worry.)

🐦 I'm temporarily out of my mind.

RATIONALIZATIONS FOR
NOT HAVING CHILDREN

🐸 I couldn't handle getting vomit on my Armani wardrobe.

🐸 My goldfish would get jealous.

🐸 I can't deal with screaming brats—especially if they're mine.

🐸 I'm not getting along with my husband. (Hopefully this is just a phase.)

🐸 It would give my in-laws another excuse to come over.

🐸 Every kid should have a pet and I hate animals.

🐸 It'll be just another person to give me the flu.

🐸 Barney *really* annoys me.

🐸 My husband and I will no longer be able to have spontaneous sex. (Not that we ever do, but I like to keep my options open.)

RATIONALIZATIONS FOR
CHOOSING NATURAL CHILDBIRTH

- I'm into pain.

- I want my husband to feel guilty.

- If pioneer women did it, so can I.

- After being married for ten years, this should be a cinch.

- It's cheaper.

- I've seen it on TV and it didn't look *that* bad.

- I want to belong to the New Age movement.

- My insurance only covers extremely painful procedures.

RATIONALIZATIONS FOR
CHOOSING TOTALLY
MEDICATED CHILDBIRTH

- I missed Woodstock.

- I tried pain once and decided I didn't like it.

- I don't want my husband to see me without makeup and sweating.

- Hey, this is the nineties. I don't have to deal with pain if I don't want to.

- I want to be able to stay in the hospital longer and be pampered.

- If they give me an episiotomy, I don't want to know about it.

- It's the civilized thing to do.

- Isn't natural childbirth for vegetarians?

- Being married to my husband is painful enough.

RATIONALIZATIONS FOR
CHEATING ON YOUR SPOUSE

🐦 It must have been the Prozac.

🐦 I don't believe in divorce.

🐦 He can't handle my vibrator and that is just unacceptable.

🐦 After trying out 22 therapists, I finally found one who would say this was a good way to figure out whether I should stay in my marriage or not.

🐦 It was a hot summer day and my nineteen-year-old yard man's muscles were glistening with sweat—what choice did I have?

🐦 I had to find out if my husband is as big as he says he is.

🐦 I don't consider having sex with my first husband "cheating."

🐦 I'm practicing to be a better lover.

🐦 I read *Cosmopolitan.*

RATIONALIZATIONS FOR
GETTING DIVORCED

- I'm no longer fascinated by a small penis.

- Now that his mistress has moved in, there's just not enough space in the bathroom.

- Now that his boyfriend had moved in, there's not enough space in the kitchen.

- I'll finally be able to go out and buy that gas-powered vibrator.

- My husband was able to find someone foolish enough to cook, clean, and have sex on demand—now it's my turn.

- He won't get out of jail until 2029.

- He was starting to look like my father.

- He refused to trim his nose hairs.

- He gave me a gift certificate to K-Mart for our anniversary. Need I say more?

RATIONALIZATIONS FOR
NOT GETTING DIVORCED

- The house and car are in his name, the kids are in mine.

- The sex isn't great, but at least there's plenty of it.

- I might have to go out and get a job.

- Affairs are more thrilling.

- He actually knows how to program the VCR.

- He has more money than anyone else I know.

- He likes my tuna casserole.

- I don't have to worry about him having affairs because I have him convinced that he's impotent with everyone else but me.

- I don't want to give my mother the opportunity to say "I told you so."

RATIONALIZATIONS FOR
SLEEPING WITH YOUR EX

- ❧ I needed to remind myself how much I hated it.

- ❧ I wanted to remind him of what he gave up.

- ❧ I can handle it (sure).

- ❧ He was pitiful and my mothering instincts kicked in.

- ❧ My vibrator was broken.

- ❧ I had just done a seminar on "letting go" and he was the perfect testing ground.

- ❧ I was ten pounds thinner and my butt looked great—I really wanted him to see this.

- ❧ I momentarily forgot what a scum he is.

- ❧ I thought I should share my "minor infection" with him.

RATIONALIZATIONS FOR
DATING YOUR FRIEND'S EX-HUSBAND

🐌 I didn't want her as a friend anyway.

🐌 She told me what a big penis he had and I wanted to see for myself.

🐌 I've always had a hard time saying no.

🐌 I'm doing research on how strong bonds are between friends.

🐌 In a town with a population of 312, he was the only man under 65 who wasn't related to me.

🐌 At least we'll have something in common.

🐌 He was really *my* boyfriend first.

🐌 I'm going through my hedonistic stage.

🐌 He was there.

RATIONALIZATIONS FOR
GETTING MARRIED AGAIN

🐚 I've given up poverty.

🐚 It couldn't be any worse than the last three times.

🐚 What's the big deal? You just say "I do" and then you can always say "I don't."

🐚 I like to change my china pattern every four years.

🐚 Those 900 numbers are getting pretty expensive.

🐚 I'm a creature of habit.

🐚 I miss the smell of dirty socks and stale beer.

🐚 It's been too long since I've been to Vegas.

🐚 It'll force me to divorce my first husband.

RATIONALIZATIONS FOR
YELLING AT YOUR SPOUSE

- He was breathing too loudly.

- His clothes didn't match.

- He leaves his dishes in the sink (and then says "they're soaking").

- When I order dessert, he says, "Do you really think you should eat that?"

- I didn't like him that day.

- I actually hated him that day.

- I have to *tell* him to take out the trash.

- He forgot Valentine's Day.

- He forgot my birthday.

- He forgot our anniversary.

- He forgot we were married.

3

HAVING IT ALL?

*"Lord, won't you buy me
a Mercedes-Benz,
My friends all drive Porches,
I must make amends."*

— JANIS JOPLIN

RATIONALIZATIONS FOR
GETTING A LIBERAL ARTS DEGREE

- People will think I'm really intelligent.

- I get to read T.S. Elliot instead of statistics.

- The guys are more sensitive.

- I'll get to have an utterly useless but impressive-looking document to hang on my wall.

- I'll be "well-rounded."

- I can con my teachers because I'm so good with words.

- I wanted to mortify my parents by spending $100,000 of their money on a degree in eighteenth-century West Indian Literature.

- I can pretend to be Sharon Stone and shake up my professors.

RATIONALIZATIONS FOR
TAKING A JOB

🐦 The guy who interviewed me was a knockout.

🐦 It gives me an excuse to get a car phone.

🐦 They have a cappuccino machine in the lunch room.

🐦 They have a great maternity plan. (Of course, I forgot to mention I was two months pregnant.)

🐦 I needed to find some way to pay for my new fur coat.

🐦 I get to be the boss of ten people. (I love control.)

🐦 A lot of good-looking attorneys work in the same building.

🐦 I lied on my resume and they believed me.

🐦 I'm broke and I ran out of excuses.

RATIONALIZATIONS FOR
BEING LATE FOR WORK

- My cat threw up.

- My gerbil died.

- I had an appointment with my Hindu monk seer.

- I was having a great dream about re-decorating my 10,000-square-foot man-sion.

- I picked up a hitchhiker and he made me take him to Las Vegas.

- I didn't realize it was daylight savings time.

- I was having a nightmare and I couldn't get away.

- I couldn't do a thing with my hair.

- I was writing down ideas for my life story and lost track of time.

- I thought I was sick . . . it turned out I wasn't.

RATIONALIZATIONS FOR
PLAYING HOOKY

- ❧ I didn't finish my project before the deadline.

- ❧ I got drunk and shaved my head the night before. (I was having a moment.)

- ❧ Oprah's guest was Kevin Costner. Need I say more?

- ❧ They were having a 50% off sale at my favorite store.

- ❧ I had sex with my boss the night before.

- ❧ I *dreamed* I had sex with my boss the night before.

- ❧ I got smashed at the company party and did a strip tease to Paul Anka's "You're Having My Baby."

- ❧ My cats need more companionship.

- ❧ I'm working from home today.

RATIONALIZATIONS FOR
WORKING LATE

🐌 I don't have a life anyway, so I might as well.

🐌 My husband's having another bout of impotence, so what's the point?

🐌 I'm trying to accumulate enough comp time for a one month trip to the psych ward.

🐌 My husband thinks I'm having an affair with my partner. I might as well give him something to worry about.

🐌 I'm the only one in this skyscraper at night and I can pretend it's all mine.

🐌 It's either that or go home to my husband.

🐌 My dog asked for more time alone.

RATIONALIZATIONS FOR
NOT WORKING LATE

- I don't want to be caught alone with my perverted boss.

- It's only a job, not brain surgery.

- I think my husband's having an affair and I want to catch him in the act.

- If I work late, I won't get home until late, then I'll eat late and get fat—no way.

- Happy Hour is only from 5:00–7:00 P.M.

- Working late would mean something ridiculous like I want to get ahead—I'm an underachiever and proud of it.

- I work at the post office.

- They couldn't pay me enough.

- I'm already on my sixth marriage.

- It's hard enough pretending to accomplish something for eight hours every day.

RATIONALIZATIONS FOR
TAKING A VACATION

- ❧ My rich uncle's about to kick the bucket and I think I'm in his will.

- ❧ My boyfriend said he'd pay for the whole thing. (I guess I can handle a small penis for a weekend.)

- ❧ My in-laws are coming to town.

- ❧ The last time I went on vacation was a month ago.

- ❧ I want to experience UFOs in Sedona.

- ❧ I can get a 20% discount on my china pattern in London if I pick it up personally.

- ❧ I need to renew my marriage.

- ❧ I need to end my marriage.

RATIONALIZATIONS FOR
LOSING A JOB

- ❧ I was ready to look for a new job anyway.

- ❧ Change is good for people.

- ❧ My boss has a mental problem and no one has figured it out yet.

- ❧ The girl who sat next to me had stinky feet.

- ❧ I hated the offices—they were painted vomit green.

- ❧ They wouldn't let me have two-hour lunches or an expense account.

- ❧ Now I can start a family and not feel guilty about leaving my career.

- ❧ I slept with my boss.

- ❧ I didn't sleep with my boss.

RATIONALIZATIONS FOR
QUITTING A JOB

- I was having PMS and my boss really pissed me off.

- They told me I couldn't wear fingernail polish to work—it's the principle.

- My boss hates women. (He hated his mother.)

- They wouldn't give me Groundhog's Day off.

- They wouldn't give me a car phone.

- My new manager is fifteen years younger than me.

- My genius was stifled.

- My industry is going through a change and I'm not.

- I was becoming far too successful.

- The plot was thickening on my soap opera.

RATIONALIZATIONS FOR
NOT ACCEPTING A PROMOTION

🐦 I'd be too visible.

🐦 I'd have to travel and stay in Motel 6's alone.

🐦 I'd have to deal with my department's finances. (Hell, I can't even balance my own checkbook.)

🐦 "Overachievement" is not in my vocabulary.

🐦 I never wanted to be a superwoman.

🐦 I'd have to wear hose every day.

🐦 I'd be expected to hobnob with the "suits."

🐦 I'd have to be at work two hours earlier.

🐦 They might expect me to work harder.

RATIONALIZATIONS FOR
STARTING YOUR OWN BUSINESS

🐦 If I'm going to slave for 60 hours a week, I'm going to do it for my own benefit.

🐦 I want to be able to tell other people what to do.

🐦 I need a tax shelter.

🐦 I'll finally get an American Express card.

🐦 I get to hire all the studly young bucks I want to fulfill my whims of fantasy.

🐦 I get to write off all my extravagant dinners, unnecessary limos, and totally outrageous weekend "business" trips to Tokyo.

🐦 I get to work out of my house and not worry about taking a shower, much less putting on make-up.

🐦 It beats collecting scraps of aluminum foil.

RATIONALIZATIONS FOR
BEING AN ACTRESS

🐸 I'll get fan mail.

🐸 I'll only have to work a few months every year.

🐸 I'll get to throw a tantrum and everyone will put up with it because they won't want to stifle my creativity.

🐸 I'll be in all of Rob Lowe's videos.

🐸 I'll get to spend hundreds of dollars on photos of myself and nobody can accuse me of vanity.

🐸 Even though there is only a .000001% chance I'll make it—I'm sure it will happen to me.

🐸 I'll have a lot of personal assistants to take care of all the annoying details of my life—like my husband and kids.

🐸 I'll get to see Michael Douglas naked.

RATIONALIZATIONS FOR
BEING AN IRS AUDITOR

- 🐸 I'll never get audited.

- 🐸 If I do get audited, I'll have connections in high places.

- 🐸 I'll get total respect.

- 🐸 People will always take me seriously

- 🐸 I'm just trying to help my country and I feel good about that.

- 🐸 I'll get to criticize other people's lifestyle.

- 🐸 My personal finances will be totally organized.

- 🐸 People will fear me.

- 🐸 People will have to be nice to me.

- 🐸 I can intimidate Mike Wallace.

- 🐸 My lovers will do everything I tell them to.

RATIONALIZATIONS FOR
BEING A LAWYER

🐛 I'll get to criticize "L.A. Law" and sound like I know what I'm talking about.

🐛 I'll have tons of friends (mostly because they want cheap advice).

🐛 I'll get a corner office with a view.

🐛 I'll get to be around a lot of good-looking professional men.

🐛 I'll get to stay in school for three extra years before facing the real world.

🐛 I'll always win arguments.

🐛 I'll be able to tell my boyfriend I'm working late and he'll believe me.

🐛 When I threaten the car mechanic that I'll sue, he'll know to take me seriously

🐛 I can legally break all laws.

🐛 Being a bitch will be an asset.

RATIONALIZATIONS FOR
BEING A PLASTIC SURGEON

🐌 Six-figure salary—need I say more?

🐌 I'll get to meet all kinds of celebrities.

🐌 I can get my butt tucked for free.

🐌 I'll never have to worry about my penmanship.

🐌 People will think I'm "godlike."

🐌 I will never look a day over 40 (not that there's anything wrong with that).

🐌 I'll get to stay dressed while looking at naked people.

🐌 I'll get great drugs.

🐌 I will be one with the "beautiful people."

RATIONALIZATIONS FOR
BEING A PROSTITUTE

🐌 This body cost me a fortune, it's time to start earning it back.

🐌 I get to look at a lot of penises and compare.

🐌 Two words: "Pretty Woman."

🐌 I'm experimenting with new ways to meet men.

🐌 I'm a nymphomaniac.

🐌 It's not my fault, it's my parents' fault and no, I don't want to talk about it.

🐌 I'm in Hollywood and working on my acting technique.

🐌 It's the only way one person can influence a politician.

🐌 A body is a terrible thing to waste.

RATIONALIZATIONS FOR
BEING A THERAPIST

🐚 I'll get to hear other people's problems and mine won't seem so bad.

🐚 It's a constant source of juicy gossip.

🐚 I'll know exactly how to drive my husband crazy.

🐚 People will pay me outrageous sums of money to just listen to their problems and say things like "this stems from your childhood," "I understand your pain," "It's not your fault," and "Uh huh, uh huh, tell me more."

🐚 I can act totally off-the-wall and everyone will think I'm eccentric.

🐚 I'll get to write off a brand new couch every year.

🐚 I'll get my problems solved for free in my group therapy sessions.

🐚 They whine, therefore I am.

RATIONALIZATIONS FOR
JOINING THE MILITARY

🐾 I won't have to worry about what to wear.

🐾 I'll finally get paid for yelling at people.

🐾 I've always wanted to carry a gun.

🐾 The male to female ratio is ten to one (pretty good odds).

🐾 Housing is cheap.

🐾 What's four years?

🐾 I never could cope with the real world– not enough rules.

🐾 I love a man in uniform.

🐾 It will force me to get in shape.

RATIONALIZATIONS FOR
BEING A FULL-TIME CAREER WOMAN

🐦 Day care centers can't be *that* bad.

🐦 There is no way I'm going to let my Ph.D. go to waste.

🐦 I refuse to be doled out an allowance by my husband.

🐦 It's the only way I can justify an incredible wardrobe of Ann Taylor and Armani.

🐦 When I began to iron my husband's boxer shorts, I realized I had no choice.

🐦 It's better than facing up to the fact that I married a slug.

🐦 I get rewarded for being bitchy.

🐦 I'm my ex's boss.

🐦 83 🐦

RATIONALIZATIONS FOR
BEING AN AT-HOME MOM

🦢 I hated my perverted boss.

🦢 I don't want someone else raising my
kids and turning them into serial
killers.

🦢 I'll get to live my childhood vicariously
through my kids.

🦢 I get to pretend I'm Betty Crocker.

🦢 It's the ultimate revenge on a man.

🦢 I finally get to tell someone else what to
do.

🦢 The cute guy next door is unemployed.

RATIONALIZATIONS FOR
HAVING A CELLULAR PHONE

🐦 I can drive anywhere, anytime and feel totally safe—even to the post office.

🐦 It makes me feel like I'm rich.

🐦 I get to sleep in an extra 30 minutes because I can call my office and do business before I arrive—now I'm not "late," I'm "efficient."

🐦 I always felt stopping at a telephone booth was beneath me.

🐦 My company pays for it.

🐦 Men seem to notice me more—I'll take all the attention I can get.

🐦 My husband and I never had time just to talk. Now we can do it via our car phones—very nineties.

RATIONALIZATIONS FOR
LIVING IN NEW YORK

🐸 I'm into noise, trash, and criminals.

🐸 I can use public transit every day and feel like I'm doing my environmental part.

🐸 After the World Trade Center terrorist bombing, I feel like I'm a character in a Robert Ludlum novel.

🐸 My friends back home think I'm really glamorous (even though I live in a rathole for $2,000 a month).

🐸 It's so continental—after walking around the city, I feel like I've visited four foreign penal colonies.

🐸 I can be as off-the-wall as I want and no one will notice a thing.

🐸 I can be a rude bitch and feel right at home.

🐸 When I'm low on money, Times Square is just around the corner.

RATIONALIZATIONS FOR
LIVING IN LOS ANGELES

🐸 The sound of the helicopters spraying for the Mediterranean fruit fly reminds me of my days in Vietnam.

🐸 Sometimes when I'm having sex, the Earth really *does* move.

🐸 Where else can you find a 24-hour hair salon/therapy group and a drive-thru Ethiopian restaurant all on the same block?

🐸 So what if I have to pay double for my rent, utilities and car insurance? My poodle can get a manicure and pedicure for ten bucks.

🐸 Smog alerts are always a great excuse to be a lazy pig.

🐸 It's very exciting to live in a place where earthquakes and riots can make us the top story of the headline news. (God, this place has really destroyed my morals.)

LIVING IN FLAT LICK, NEBRASKA (POP. 812)

🐸 I'm either related to or grew up with everybody in town.

🐸 The loudest noise at night is Jim Bob howling at the moon.

🐸 They still believe in business done by a handshake.

🐸 After twelve years of school my kids will be able to read and write.

🐸 I knew if my kid got into trouble and didn't tell me, everyone else in town would.

🐸 If my husband had an affair, there's a good chance it would be with me.

RATIONALIZATIONS FOR
LIVING WITH YOUR PARENTS

🕊 I don't have to pay rent and my mother does all my laundry.

🕊 They go to bed by 10:00 P.M., so I only have to put up with them for a few hours each night.

🕊 They promised me a big inheritance if I stayed—so what's a few years of my life?

🕊 I never could get into that "work" thing.

🕊 My mother already knows how to deal with kids—I want her to deal with mine.

🕊 I'm saving—no, I don't know how long it's going to take and no, I don't want to talk about it.

🕊 I'm trying to reclaim the "child within."

🕊 I've been under house arrest since 1983.

THE BEAUTY OF
IT ALL

*"Every woman knows measurements
are statistics and statistics lie."*

— UNKNOWN

RATIONALIZATIONS FOR
GETTING BEAUTY TREATMENTS

- They were having a 50% off sale on the deep Swedish facial.

- I found my first gray hair, got stood up, and broke a nail—all in the same day.

- I needed attention.

- My mother just confused me with *her* mother.

- The masseur looks like Mel Gibson.

- I was feeling old.

- I was feeling dead.

- I wasn't feeling anything.

- My husband has been calling me Harry.

RATIONALIZATIONS FOR
GOING ON A DIET

**(There are no logical rationalizations
for this—it's pure hell!)**

RATIONALIZATIONS FOR
NOT GOING ON A DIET

- 🕊 I'm hungry.

- 🕊 I may be pregnant.

- 🕊 I'm having a PMS craving.

- 🕊 Oprah says diets don't work.

- 🕊 My thighs aren't really *that* big.

- 🕊 I'm over 30 and it's probably a lost cause anyway.

- 🕊 My husband said he likes the "Victorian" look.

- 🕊 I'm in a destructive phase.

- 🕊 My psychic said I was deprived in my past life, so I can "go for it" in this one.

- 🕊 I've got to be me.

- 🕊 I really don't *want* to look like Susan Powter.

RATIONALIZATIONS FOR
NOT WEARING MAKE-UP

🐌 I'm depressed.

🐌 I want my skin to breathe.

🐌 I'm not in a relationship.

🐌 I don't want to be in a relationship.

🐌 My husband is out of town.

🐌 I'll be around my family and no one cares what I look like.

🐌 Why put on make-up when the smog is free?

🐌 I just don't feel like it and I'm totally comfortable with my decision.

🐌 I have inner beauty.

RATIONALIZATIONS FOR
NOT WORKING OUT

🐸 It was raining so I wanted to cuddle up with my book instead.

🐸 It was sunny and I wanted to get a tan instead.

🐸 It was cloudy and I was depressed again.

🐸 There are way too many skinny people at the gym.

🐸 My workout clothes are dirty.

🐸 I had to clean my baseboards.

🐸 "Roseanne" was about to start.

🐸 My left forefinger joint was achy.

🐸 I was stressed out, so I had ice-cream instead.

🐸 I had a better offer.

RATIONALIZATIONS FOR
HAVING PLASTIC SURGERY

🐦 I live in California.

🐦 My five-year-old told me I looked like Barbara Bush.

🐦 By the time the liposuction was done, it was time to get another face lift.

🐦 My monthly facials quit working.

🐦 My weekly exercise quit working.

🐦 Everything quit working!

🐦 It gave me an excuse to go to Mexico for a month.

🐦 I'll get to date guys twenty years younger than me.

🐦 They were having a sale—get one boob done, get the other done for free.

🐦 My Prozac was wearing off.

RATIONALIZATIONS FOR
CHANGING YOUR HAIR COLOR

🐚 For a moment my sister and I thought we were Thelma and Louise—just long enough for us to go platinum blond and fire red.

🐚 I was having one of my very infrequent moments of adventure and took a picture of Sinead O'Connor to my stylist . . . . Now I'm on a first-name basis with the local wig dealer.

🐚 When I saw the two-for-one do-it-yourself hair color for seven bucks a bottle, I knew there was no turning back.

🐚 I figured no one would notice anyway (of course, that was *before* my hair turned fuchsia).

🐚 My husband thinks he's with someone new every six months.

RATIONALIZATIONS FOR
HAVING A BAD HAIR CUT

🦀 What bad hair cut?

🦀 The commercial said the home perm kit was "fool-proof."

🦀 I was abducted by aliens who needed hair samples.

🦀 My best friend said, "trust me."

🦀 At least I'm set for the next two Halloweens.

🦀 Oh well, my husband said we'd sue.

🦀 My hairdresser said her hand slipped—I will *never* forget to tip her again.

🦀 It's not so bad, is it?

RATIONALIZATIONS FOR
BEING A SLAVE TO FASHION

🐚 Now that stretch pants and moose-mama tops are in, I'm the queen of fashion.

🐚 Can I help it if I turn into the Tasmanian Devil every time I walk into a shoe store?

🐚 I heard that wearing three-inch heels would firm my thighs and define my calves. (I knew there was a reason I gave up my health club membership.)

🐚 I read that you can burn up to 300 calories trying on clothes, not to mention an extra 50 for writing the checks.

🐚 My psychic says Imelda Marcos and I were sisters in a past life.

🐚 I *enjoy* having bunions and vericose veins.

RATIONALIZATIONS FOR
NOT SHAVING YOUR LEGS

🐦 I'm not in a relationship so what difference does it make?

🐦 I'm in my "earth-momma" stage.

🐦 I'm trying to break the *Guiness Book of World Records* for the longest, narliest leg hairs.

🐦 I want to see if a weed-eater works better than a razor.

🐦 I won't have to worry about getting picked up in bars.

🐦 I'm on vacation—I can do whatever the hell I want.

🐦 I'm the man in my lesbian relationship.

🐦 The hair hides my cellulite so well that I don't even have to work out anymore.

5

EXCESSES OR BUST

*"My dear, I don't care what they do,
so long as they don't do it in the street
and frighten the horses."*

— Beatrice Stella Tanner Campbell

RATIONALIZATIONS FOR
EATING TOO MUCH

🐚 My diet starts tomorrow.

🐚 I was anorexic in my past life.

🐚 I got in a fight with my dog.

🐚 My free coupon for a Double Whopper, large fries and a Coke was about to expire.

🐚 I'd already eaten 2,000 calories by noon, so I figured I might as well keep going.

🐚 I'm rewarding myself for losing two pounds.

🐚 My therapist said my potty training was deficient.

🐚 No one was watching.

🐚 I grew up believing the four basic food groups were Mexican, Italian, French provençale, and southern deep-fried.

🐚 150 pounds sounds about right for 5'2". (Doesn't it?)

RATIONALIZATIONS FOR
EATING A QUART OF ICE CREAM IN ONE SITTING

🐤 I was depressed.

🐤 He left and I don't give a damn.

🐤 They were having a "buy five pints get ten pints free" sale. How could I resist that?

🐤 I'm pregnant and I can eat anything I want.

🐤 I'm single, I have fourteen children, and I have no prospects for a decent relationship. What the hell do you expect?

🐤 I've always felt that ice cream is healthy.

🐤 I'm a vegetarian and I need my protein.

🐤 I know a lot of men that love that voluptuous look.

🐤 I had to prove a pint did not contain four servings.

🐤 106 🐤

RATIONALIZATIONS FOR
EATING OUT ALL THE TIME

- I can't be tied to an oven.

- I cooked every day for fifteen years for my first husband—and he died!

- It always tastes so much better when someone else prepares it.

- I'm looking for Mr. Right.

- My sink is full.

- I'm stuck in the eighties.

- We never got to eat out when I was growing up.

- These people are trained professionals. I'm not.

- Cooking for one is just too depressing.

- I love to be served.

RATIONALIZATIONS FOR
DRINKING TOO MUCH

- It was Friday night drinkin' with the office crowd.

- It was Saturday night partyin' with my best friends.

- It was Sunday brunch and my mother-in-law was there.

- It was hump day (gotta get through the week).

- It was my birthday (I was really depressed).

- There was an open bar.

- I ran out of coffee, soda, and cigarettes

- It's the latest diet plan.

- My water got shut off.

RATIONALIZATIONS FOR
QUITTING SMOKING

- 🐦 I'd save $2,000 a year.

- 🐦 No one smokes in my office.

- 🐦 I won't have the smell of cigarettes in my hair and clothes to cover up my expensive perfume.

- 🐦 My husband said he'd give me $1,000 if I quit.

- 🐦 I can be one of those non-smoking snobs.

- 🐦 I'll get better tables in restaurants.

- 🐦 I won't have to worry about annoying other people when I'm out.

- 🐦 My doctor said it was either the pill or smoking, so I picked the pill.

- 🐦 I want white teeth again.

RATIONALIZATIONS FOR
NOT QUITTING SMOKING

🐦 I'll gain ten more pounds.

🐦 I have a death wish.

🐦 I love it.

🐦 I don't smoke *that* much.

🐦 I like brown teeth.

🐦 Why not enjoy my downfall?

🐦 My grandmother's brother-in-law's cousin smoked for 70 years and lived to be 95.

🐦 I only smoke when I drink.

🐦 I like annoying strangers at random.

RATIONALIZATIONS FOR
SLEEPING LATE

🐌 I'm a lazy sloth.

🐌 I guess that Valium did the trick.

🐌 I can't face another damn sunny day.

🐌 My fifth alarm didn't go off this morning.

🐌 In my dreams I'm sleeping with Kevin Costner, in reality with Cro-Magnon Man.

🐌 I had a hangover.

🐌 It was raining.

🐌 My sheets were clean.

🐌 I was having a great dream about my incredible love affair with the richest man in the world.

🐌 My cat was asleep on my stomach and I didn't want to disturb her.

RATIONALIZATIONS FOR
HAVING A MAID

- ❧ I don't know how to work my vacuum cleaner and I want to keep it that way.

- ❧ I'll break my nails and they cost twenty bucks a week.

- ❧ There's always somebody there to sign for my packages.

- ❧ I'm helping my maid support her ten children and her disabled husband.

- ❧ My social life is much too busy for me to worry about insignificant things like a clean house.

- ❧ I love coming home to the smell of Pine-Sol.

- ❧ My animals have a companion.

- ❧ She always tells me I look great.

- ❧ Now I'm not the only one spurning my husband's advances.

RATIONALIZATIONS FOR
NOT DOING HOUSEWORK

🐛 It'll just get dirty again.

🐛 The roaches need to eat, too.

🐛 No one ever comes over anyway.

🐛 Filth makes me creative.

🐛 I want to see how long my husband will go without lifting a finger.

🐛 I'm trying to get over my compulsive need to clean.

🐛 It'll mess up my hair.

🐛 Being a slob is eccentric.

🐛 I'll do it tomorrow.

🐛 I'll do it next week.

🐛 I'll do it next month.

🐛 I'll move.

RATIONALIZATIONS FOR
NOT DOING YARD WORK

🐦 It'll grow back anyway.

🐦 I'm trying to piss off my neighbors.

🐦 I like the jungle look.

🐦 I'm conserving water (my lawn is dead).

🐦 The kids are playing hide and go seek (in the grass).

🐦 I'm out of lemonade.

🐦 The weeds are about to bloom.

🐦 Everything freezes during the winter anyway.

🐦 The nursery guy said these plants were very low maintenance.

🐦 I hate the color green.

RATIONALIZATIONS FOR
NOT RECYCLING

🐌 I don't have enough room for all those containers.

🐌 My dog always chews up newspapers that are sitting around and it's too big a mess.

🐌 I didn't know that recycling was "in."

🐌 I don't know where the recycling center is.

🐌 The recycling center is too far away.

🐌 The recycling center is never open the hours I need to go.

🐌 Maybe the Earth *likes* plastic.

6

THE EMOTIONAL ROLLERCOASTER

"Life's a bitch—or is it beach?"

— UNKNOWN

RATIONALIZATIONS FOR
BEING A BITCH

- Because I goddamn feel like it!

- She started it.

- It's not my fault, it runs in my family.

- I refuse to be accountable for my actions for at least five days every month.

- All the real bitches seem to get ahead, so I thought I'd give it a shot.

- I know people already think I'm a bitch, so why not act the part?

- So I slept with my best friends' husbands and cut in front of pregnant women in line at the grocery store— what's the big deal?

- My therapist says "venting" is healthy.

- Everyone needs a hobby.

RATIONALIZATIONS FOR
GOING TO THERAPY

🐸 I just turned 30 and this seemed like the next logical step.

🐸 It's the nineties thing to do.

🐸 It's a great way to meet wimpy, messed-up men.

🐸 I want to be self-actualized. (I don't know what it means, but I like the way it sounds.)

🐸 My husband left me for a younger woman, my kid joined a cult, and my dog stopped taking me seriously.

🐸 It was either therapy, shock treatments, or jail—not a hard choice.

🐸 I can talk and talk and they have to listen.

🐸 I have access to an unlimited supply of Prozac.

RATIONALIZATIONS FOR
NOT GOING TO THERAPY

🐢 I don't want to meet my inner child. (I'm sure she's a snot-nosed little brat.)

🐢 I'm perfect and I want to be alone.

🐢 I don't take criticism well.

🐢 Why should I pay someone to point out my faults? What I don't know won't hurt me.

🐢 Expressing my feelings is not a problem. When I cry, I get what I want.

🐢 I don't want to forgive myself, my parents, their parents or the gas station attendant.

🐢 Having a crisis once a month keeps my life exciting.

🐢 I'm into denial (and I want to stay that way).

🐢 Let the chips fall where they may.

RATIONALIZATIONS FOR
FEELING DEPRESSED

- I broke a nail.

- My cat threw up on my new Oriental rug.

- My husband told me he is gay.

- It's too damned sunny outside.

- My best friend told me I have bad breath.

- My therapist said he can't deal with me anymore.

- I've gotten five phone calls over the last month suggesting I should go to my doctor and get "the test."

- I got a flat tire on the highway, and the only person to stop and help me looked like Charles Manson.

- My parrot was diagnosed as a schizophrenic.

- My new boyfriend said he knew of ways to help me with my cellulite.

RATIONALIZATIONS FOR
NOT FEELING GUILTY

🕊 It's not my fault.

🕊 I believe it's every woman for herself.

🕊 Guilt is not in my vocabulary.

🕊 Spending $1,000 on bathroom acces-
sories seems reasonable to me.

🕊 My life is hell and everyone should feel
sorry for me.

🕊 My affair is only temporary—it doesn't
mean anything—my husband thinks I'm
androgynous—I'm temporarily insane—
I'm thinking, I'm thinking . . . .

🕊 My mother is guilty enough for both of
us.

🕊 I'm an atheist.

🕊 I'm too poor to feel guilty.

RATIONALIZATIONS FOR
BEING A HYPOCHONDRIAC

🐸 I get lots of attention.

🐸 I make my kids feel guilty and then they come see me.

🐸 I always have a reason not to have sex.

🐸 My having a near-death experience three times a year keeps my husband on his toes.

🐸 I have a mad crush on my doctor.

🐸 After seeing 1,000 commercials a day for Pepto Bismol, Preparation H, and Monastat 7, what the hell do you expect?

🐸 When I go to the hospital, everyone knows my name and they wait on me hand and foot.

🐸 It's the only way I can get my husband to act like he cares about me.

🐸 People expect things when you're healthy.

A RANDOM TOUCH

*"What else is there to say
but everything."*

— GWENDOLYN BROOKS

RATIONALIZATIONS FOR
NOT HAVING PEOPLE OVER
FOR DINNER

- 🐸 I'd have to clean my house.

- 🐸 My china doesn't match.

- 🐸 I'd have to pretend my husband and I like each other.

- 🐸 I don't have a dishwasher.

- 🐸 My kitchen is too small.

- 🐸 I can't cook and I'm not willing to admit it.

- 🐸 I'd have to put on makeup.

- 🐸 I don't have enough chairs.

- 🐸 I'd have to move all those dead bodies.

RATIONALIZATIONS FOR
NOT GOING OUT

🐌 I don't want to put on make-up.

🐌 I don't want to put on pantyhose.

🐌 I have a zit.

🐌 I just ordered pizza.

🐌 The guy I met last month might call.

🐌 I have diarrhea.

🐌 I can't put my book down.

🐌 I don't have a thing to wear.

🐌 I broke a nail.

🐌 There's a clearance sale on the Home
Shopping Network tonight.

RATIONALIZATIONS FOR
JOINING THE NEW AGE MOVEMENT

- 🕊 I get to rationalize not being successful during this lifetime because there is always the next lifetime.

- 🕊 I get to wear crystal jewelry and people think I'm deep.

- 🕊 It confirmed that my husband was my mother-in-law in a past life.

- 🕊 It confirmed that my boss was Hannibal the Cannibal in a past life.

- 🕊 I'll get to meet my higher self. (I'll bet she's great!)

- 🕊 Instead of finding a successful career, I get to find myself.

- 🕊 It validates my 1965 UFO experience.

- 🕊 If Shirley MacLaine believes in it, then so do I.

RATIONALIZATIONS FOR
NOT JOINING THE
NEW AGE MOVEMENT

- 🐚 I don't like to travel, whether I'm in my body or out of it.

- 🐚 I bet the people who buy crystals are the same ones who bought pet rocks.

- 🐚 I've become accustomed to being the victim.

- 🐚 I wouldn't be able to make other people feel guilty anymore.

- 🐚 Have you ever met a *real* man who's into the New Age?

- 🐚 I think I'd have a really hard time not being judgmental of others.

- 🐚 I don't want to be held accountable for every little thing I do.

- 🐚 I never did like Shirley MacLaine.

- 🐚 I'm already perfect.

RATIONALIZATIONS FOR
NOT BUYING A PRESENT

🐚 She's a bitch.

🐚 She didn't buy *me* one.

🐚 I just couldn't find the right thing so I didn't get anything.

🐚 I think a card is just fine.

🐚 I don't believe in forced giving.

🐚 The shipping costs are too expensive.

🐚 I'd have to wrap it.

🐚 I don't know her *that* well.

🐚 My credit cards were maxed out.

🐚 I probably won't get a present in return, so what's the point?

RATIONALIZATIONS FOR
MAKING PHONE CALLS AT 2:00 A.M.

🐦 I was crying and I didn't know why.

🐦 I dreamed the grocer was Satan and he made me drop to my knees and pray at the checkout counter. It freaked me out and I just *had* to talk about it!

🐦 I heard a noise in the bathroom.

🐦 I drank sixteen cups of coffee today and sleep was out of the question.

🐦 I just finished reading Stephen King.

🐦 I was watching "Midnight Psychiatry" on TV and I think there is something really wrong with me.

🐦 I didn't want to eat a whole package of Oreos alone.

🐦 I thought the three-hour time difference was earlier instead of later. (Oops!)

RATIONALIZATIONS FOR
OWNING A CAT

- They're quiet.

- You can go away for an entire week and they'll be fine.

- You don't have to walk them.

- Their food is cheap.

- The cat hair matches my couch.

- They don't vomit *that* often.

- If they fall three stories, they usually live.

- They're satisfied with the fact that their entire world is made up of a 1,200-square-foot apartment.

- They give my furniture a sort of post-modern, scratchy look.

- Cat therapy costs less than dog therapy.

RATIONALIZATIONS FOR
OWNING A DOG

🐾 He's my best friend.

🐾 He's my only friend.

🐾 He forces me to exercise.

🐾 I no longer need a garbage disposal.

🐾 He's always happy to see me when I come home (unlike my husband).

🐾 He never criticizes me.

🐾 I can tell him anything.

🐾 I don't have to change his diapers.

🐾 He's cheaper than an alarm system.

🐾 He fertilizes the lawn.

RATIONALIZATIONS FOR
OWNING A
BOA CONSTRICTOR

- Slithering is very soothing.

- My in-laws don't come over anymore.

- The IRS auditor is totally willing to allow all of our deductions.

- For some reason my landlord never minds if my rent is late.

- I never have to worry about bad dates hanging around too long.

- My boyfriend thinks it's real sexy.

- It's cheap pest control.

- I no longer have to concern myself with that pesky mongoose.

RATIONALIZATIONS FOR
BEING A VEGETARIAN

- I can eat ten times a day and not gain an ounce.

- I don't have to exercise anymore.

- I can have a dinner party for eight for under twenty bucks.

- My boss is into the New Age so I thought I'd brown-nose and give it a shot.

- People never want to come over for dinner.

- I'm never asked to bring anything.

- Men hate it and I hate men.

- I can drink and smoke as much as I want because I'm eating well.

RATIONALIZATIONS FOR
BEING A HARE KRISHNA

- ❧ I never have to wash my hair.

- ❧ I love the "sheet" look.

- ❧ It's a great excuse not to work.

- ❧ My parents are Catholic.

- ❧ I'm a natural at being annoying.

- ❧ I can eat all I want and wear a muumuu.

- ❧ People think I've gone off the deep end and don't bother me anymore.

- ❧ I'm into community living.

- ❧ I get letters from George Harrison.

- ❧ I like airports.

RATIONALIZATIONS FOR
BEING AN AGNOSTIC

➤ I don't have to decide if I don't want to.

➤ I really don't believe, but . . . just in case.

➤ I can still believe and not have to go to church.

➤ I still get invited to holiday parties.

➤ Evolution makes an awful lot of sense.

➤ I don't have to give but I can still receive.

➤ I can participate in religious conversations and annoy people by not taking sides.

➤ I want to be able to sin and not feel bad about it.

➤ I like keeping my options open.

RATIONALIZATIONS FOR
BEING AN ATHEIST

🐦 I like to sleep in on Sundays.

🐦 I save money by not donating to the church.

🐦 If I can't see it, I don't believe it.

🐦 I don't want to do unto others as they do unto me.

🐦 If someone messes around with my husband, I'm gonna kill them and not feel bad about it.

🐦 Look at a chimpanzee, then look at Andy Rooney—need I say more?

🐦 I suffer enough in this world.

🐦 I don't need to validate my existence.

🐦 I believe in wealth, power, and greed.

🐦 If there were a God, it would be me.

RATIONALIZATIONS FOR
CALLING YOUR PARENTS

🐌 I'm depressed and I want to wallow in it.

🐌 I'm broke.

🐌 I had to tell my mom what a jerk my husband was the other day.

🐌 I needed a character reference for a job—well, they know me better than anyone—hmm, that may be bad.

🐌 I needed bail.

🐌 They've left twenty messages on my machine in the last week—I guess it's time.

🐌 They've got a new 800 number; now I have no excuse not to call, and it's free, so what the heck.

🐌 They're suing me for duress over their lifetime—I have no choice.

🐌 They're drawing up their will.

RATIONALIZATIONS FOR
NOT CALLING YOUR PARENTS

🐾 I've gone into hiding.

🐾 I'm depressed and I don't want it to get worse than it already is.

🐾 My phone's not working—for some reason it just won't call their town.

🐾 I'd rather be right than happy.

🐾 They've just never understood me—my life, my cult, my shaved head, my nose rings, my . . .

🐾 Why would I want to talk to someone who's hysterical, critical, depressing, and totally out of touch with reality, and reminds me exactly of myself?

🐾 I'm trying to save money.

🐾 My medication makes dialing impossible.

🐾 I don't stick pins in my eyes, either.

RATIONALIZATIONS FOR
CELEBRATING YOUR BIRTHDAY

🐸 It's a great reason to get smashed.

🐸 I get lots of "stuff."

🐸 Everyone has to be nice to me. (Finally!)

🐸 *I* was born—why shouldn't everybody celebrate?

🐸 I never had birthday parties when I was a kid so I'm damn well going to do it now.

🐸 It's a great way to spend money and not feel one ounce of guilt.

🐸 It's a great reason to go out, pig out, and not work out.

🐸 I must celebrate the one day I gave my mother more grief than she gave me.

RATIONALIZATIONS FOR
NOT CELEBRATING YOUR BIRTHDAY

❧ I celebrate *every* day.

❧ Maybe if I pretend it's not my birthday, it will just go away.

❧ I have no friends.

❧ I don't believe in time.

❧ If I can't have what I want, I don't want anything at all. (All I want is a Jag.)

❧ I gave up celebrating my birthday for Lent (it seemed like the wise thing to do since I don't have a life).

❧ What's the point? Somewhere in the world someone else is celebrating for me.

❧ Why celebrate more wrinkles and sags?

❧ My heart could not take the excitement.

RATIONALIZATIONS FOR
LETTING YOUR PLANTS DIE

🐸 I have two brown thumbs.

🐸 The last time I talked to them, they sassed me.

🐸 They're cheap, so I just keep buying more.

🐸 Dead, decaying matter works well with my decor.

🐸 My ex-boyfriend gave them to me—let 'em rot in hell.

🐸 Who knew they wouldn't like scotch?

🐸 So I'm not a horticulturist, but I'm great in bed.

🐸 I forgot to pay my water bill.

🐸 I thought they were plastic.

🐸 They're all my cats get to eat.

RATIONALIZATIONS FOR
MOVING ACROSS THE COUNTRY

- My mother and her obnoxious seventeenth husband are driving me crazy.

- Alaska can't be *that* bad. (Maybe I'll meet a horny young Eskimo.)

- I was on a business trip and met Mr. Right—it's time to leave Mr. Wrong behind.

- Isn't the grass always greener?

- My psychic told me I'd meet my wealthy husband-to-be in El Paso and I just *had* to go fulfill my destiny.

- It's cheaper than paying off all my parking tickets.

- It's a convenient way to end a relationship.

- There are no more potential sexual partners within a 100-mile radius.

RATIONALIZATIONS FOR
SEEING YOUR IN-LAWS

🐸 There are only so many times we can pretend we're not home and get away with it.

🐸 We want to be left in their will.

🐸 They give us money every time we see them.

🐸 It's a free home-cooked meal.

🐸 They do our laundry.

🐸 I get to hear dirt on my husband that I never knew about.

🐸 They refuse to let me help in the kitchen.

🐸 They have a pool and a big-screen TV.

🐸 They can afford heat.

RATIONALIZATIONS FOR
NOT SEEING YOUR IN-LAWS

- 🦆 I'd have to wear that purple and orange polka dot sweater they gave me for Christmas.

- 🦆 I'd have to act pleasant for hours on end.

- 🦆 I'd have to clean my ceiling fans and my pantry shelves. (Gross.)

- 🦆 They think I'm unworthy because I refuse to join the Adult Children with Exceptional In-Laws Association.

- 🦆 They cut my daughter's hair and I cannot forgive them.

- 🦆 I just saw them yesterday.

- 🦆 I just saw them ten years ago.

- 🦆 They think I stole their son. (Lucky for him.)

RATIONALIZATIONS FOR
STAYING HOME ON A SATURDAY NIGHT

🐚 My car was repossessed by MasterCard.

🐚 I'm married—what's the point?

🐚 It's the Brady Bunch marathon weekend.

🐚 I'm depressed and I want to have a good cry with my cats.

🐚 I told him I couldn't see him until he decided to commit, so it's another Saturday night gone to hell. (Being strong sucks.)

🐚 I'm chanting with my Buddhist neighbors.

🐚 I'm afraid of running into the man I can't remember being with last Saturday night.

RATIONALIZATIONS FOR
NOT STAYING HOME ON A SATURDAY NIGHT

- My house is infested with fleas.

- My husband's out of town—so I'm taking advantage of the opportunity.

- Those Buddhist chanters next door are too damn loud.

- I don't want to be here when my mother calls.

- I will *not* be stood up.

- I can't deal with another night of reruns and MTV.

- My horoscope said a meteor is due to land on my apartment.

RATIONALIZATIONS FOR
READING SELF-HELP BOOKS

🐸 It's cheaper than a psychologist.

🐸 I'm working on calming the beast within.

🐸 I want to attract men who do not have webbed feet.

🐸 My friends think I have a truly examined life.

🐸 I'm trying to figure out why I'm unemployed, in love with a Hell's Angel, and can't stand my next door neighbor.

🐸 We haven't had sex in three months. (I'll try anything at this point.)

🐸 It keeps me from watching "Men Who Dress Up Like Mother Goose and the Women Who Love Them" on Oprah.

🐸 Eating them didn't help.

RATIONALIZATIONS FOR
READING WOMEN'S MAGAZINES

🐛 They scare the hell out of my husband.

🐛 They reinforce the fact that my sex life really does stink.

🐛 The article on "How to Have a Cindy Crawford Butt in Five Days or Less" was absolutely essential.

🐛 I read them when I'm really depressed and want to feel even worse.

🐛 They have these great "relationship tests" that I force my boyfriend to take with me and prove how I'm right and he's a lazy, selfish pig.

🐛 If I can't buy my wardrobe from Armani and Chanel, I want to at least be able to see what I'm missing.

RATIONALIZATIONS FOR
TRAVELING ALONE

🐦 No one else wants to go to Bangladesh.

🐦 It's my money, it's my time—I can do whatever the hell I want.

🐦 I figure if I travel around the world, I'm bound to meet the man of my dreams. (Of course, he may not be able to speak English, but who needs small talk?)

🐦 Life in Hoboken, New Jersey is quickly losing its glamour.

🐦 I'm 30, have two kids, live in the suburbs, and have bad hair, and my husband has put on 40 pounds. Can you blame me?

🐦 After seeing an 85-year-old man bungee jump off a hot-air balloon, I ran out of excuses.

🐦 The only people I know who would travel with me are in a home for the terminally strange.

RATIONALIZATIONS FOR
NOT REMEMBERING YOUR DREAMS

- 🐸 I don't really *want* to remember what my boss looks like naked.

- 🐸 It'll save a fortune in analyst's fees.

- 🐸 I'd just end up telling people about them and then they'd know what a pervert I am.

- 🐸 I'll have an even harder time differentiating between fantasy and reality.

- 🐸 I don't want to be forced to give up Chocolate Orgasm ice cream before bed.

- 🐸 I might decide that I look good in green hair.

- 🐸 I might actually attempt to have sex with five men and a panda.

- 🐸 If my dreams are pleasant, I'll have one more reason not to get out of bed.

RATIONALIZATIONS FOR
PROCRASTINATING

🐸 I'll do it later.

🐸 In the grand scheme of things, what will it *really* matter?

🐸 My Hindu monk seer said that large, green aliens are going to invade the earth soon, so why bother?

🐸 Flossing is a higher priority.

🐸 I'm too busy to worry about details.

🐸 Dammit—it's time I started putting myself first.

🐸 I'm already so far behind that there's not really much point in getting all worked up about it.

🐸 *Seinfeld* is on.

🐸 It can wait (I hope).

🐸 As long as I don't get fired, what's the big deal?

RATIONALIZATIONS FOR
IGNORING TRAFFIC LAWS

🐸 My iguana was in labor and I had to get to the vet's office *fast*.

🐸 Hey, I pay my taxes.

🐸 I'm trying to be more like a man.

🐸 With all the drugs in my system, stopping could have been risky.

🐸 I just got back from two months in Mexico.

🐸 Hey, I'm a cab driver—it's expected.

🐸 I'm practicing for the Indy 500.

🐸 The tunes were rockin' and I was rollin'.

🐸 I've been through childbirth, so death does not scare me.

RATIONALIZATIONS FOR
GETTING PULLED OVER

🐦 My odometer must be broken.

🐦 If it can happen to Letterman, it can happen to anyone.

🐦 I don't remember learning *anything* in driving school about having to keep all four wheels on the ground.

🐦 I thought the ambulance driver wanted to drag race—*really.*

🐦 I'm wallpapering my bathroom with traffic tickets and I needed a few more.

🐦 The cop was extremely cute and I just *had* to meet him.

🐦 My favorite store was having an outrageous sale. I'm saving a fortune, so who cares about one measly ticket?

🐦 How can I be expected to read all of those signs while in the throes of orgasm?

🐦 I'm having PMS and I don't give a damn.

RATIONALIZATIONS FOR
ALL OTHER OCCASIONS

Note: If you can't find a rationalization to apply to your specific situation, try using one from the list below. These will work for almost anything.

- I was depressed.

- I was PMS-ing.

- It's an investment.

- I have to love myself before I can love anyone else.

- I can't stand my in-laws (past, present or future).

- I work at the post office.

- I'm into denial (and I want to stay that way).

- I needed bail.

- It's a free country.

- Why not?

About the Authors

A native of Enid, Oklahoma, **Allison McCune** received a Bachelor's degree in television and film production from Trinity University in San Antonio, Texas. For the last ten years, she has been producing television programs for PBS and other independent clients. She is now a producer for ABC-TV in Los Angeles and lives with her two fat cats, Piper and Sophia.

Tomye Boykin Spears grew up in San Antonio, Texas. She graduated from Southern Methodist University in Dallas with a Bachelor's degree in history. She gave Los Angeles a try for six years but just couldn't rationalize it any longer. She is currently back in San Antonio, working on a Master's degree in psychology.

Readers—send us your favorite rationalizations! Mail to:

Rationalizations
Bob Adams, Inc.
260 Center Street, Holbrook MA 02343